Why Fast?

Why should we bother with fasting? After all, we're busy people. Perhaps in theory we like the idea of fasting, but in practice, we have jobs, schoolwork, families, and too many errands to run. So you're asking, why should I throw fasting into the midst of my busy life? Let's go through some reasons why fasting can be something meaningful—and not just another thing on your "to do" list.

Fasting facilitates a deeper sense of intimacy with God.

Drawing closer to our Redeemer will always help guide us through the inevitable difficulties we will encounter for the rest of our lives. We're never going to stop feeling pulled in a million directions. Our best option is to invite the Lord into every aspect of our lives and ask him to continue his work of making us holy, making us to mirror him with increasing clarity. When we choose to forego food for a time, it can remind us to set our eyes, not on what or where we're going to eat next, but on our true bread of life.

> Jesus instructed the crowds: "Do not work for food that spoils, but for food that endures to eternal life, which the Son of Man will give you." —John 6:27

> He went on to explain: "For the bread of God is the bread that comes down from heaven and gives life to the world. … I am the bread of life. Whoever comes to me will never go hungry, and whoever believes in me will never be thirsty." —John 6:33–35

Fasting reveals our weaknesses, forcing us to rely on God.

When we fast, we may feel weaker and more vulnerable. We may have strong cravings that we must resist. Everything might become a little more challenging. In this sense, fasting forces us to rely on God in a renewed way— we're driven into his arms in prayer. This reminder of our dependent nature points us toward the ultimate Sustainer.

D1447411

Why Did They Fast?	What Happened?
Aid in battle and God's guidance	The Lord delivers the other tribes of Israel against the Benjamites.
To ask God's forgiveness for their idolatry	The Lord forgives and protects Israel.
To plead for the life of his son	David's son dies.
To ask for God's forgiveness and to beseech him to restore Jerusalem and safely return the people of Israel to its borders	The Lord is with Nehemiah who asks the king to let him return to Jerusalem. He departs for Jerusalem with the king's protection.
The purpose isn't exactly specified, but it was combined with weeping and wailing in response to the edict.	Not specified
To help Esther find favor before the king, so that she could plead for the Jews.	She finds favor in the king's court, and she is able to get the king to rescind the edict.
To beg for God's forgiveness	The text doesn't specify whether the fast was actually carried out by the people of Israel. Those in power, especially the King Zedekiah, do not heed Jeremiah's warnings. Nebuchadnezzar captures Jerusalem.
In order to avoid defiling themselves with the choice foods and wine of King Nebuchadnezzar	They retain their health, are blessed with great wisdom and intelligence, and are given positions of importance in the king's court.
To beg for the Lord's forgiveness on behalf of his people	The Lord gives Daniel a prophetic vision of the future Savior.
The text doesn't identify one specific reason for this fast. However, Daniel was in mourning as a result of Israel's disconnect from God.	The Lord gives Daniel another prophetic vision.
To beg for the Lord's forgiveness in the face of Israel's impending punishment	The Lord forgives his people.
To beg for the Lord's forgiveness	The Lord relents from his plan to destroy the city, forgiving the people of Nineveh.
Not specified, but this period of fasting is situated right between Jesus' baptism and the beginning of his ministry.	He is challenged by Satan in the wilderness, and he remains strong in the face of temptation.
In order to tell the reader about her character, Luke mentions that Anna frequently fasted.	She is blessed by seeing the long-awaited Messiah in the temple as a child.
Not specified, but Paul is blind after his encounter with Christ on the Damascus road, waiting instructions from the Lord.	Paul's sight is restored, and he is filled with the Holy Spirit.
Seeking God's guidance	They receive the Lord's guidance regarding who to send out to do his will.
To raise up the leaders of the churches in Antioch, Lystra, and Iconium	Paul and Barnabas commit these leaders to the Lord.

> He humbled you, causing you to hunger and then feeding you
> with manna, which neither you nor your ancestors had known, to
> teach you that man does not live on bread alone but on every
> word that comes from the mouth of the LORD.
> —Deuteronomy 8:3

Fasting is a way of worshiping God.

When we acknowledge God as our Provider, we worship him—we praise our Creator, Redeemer, and Sustainer for his limitless power and grace—leading to that deeper sense of intimacy with the Lord.

> Jesus said: "And do not set your heart on what you will eat or
> drink; do not worry about it. For the pagan world runs after all
> such things, and your Father knows that you need them. But seek
> his kingdom, and these things will be given to you as well."
> —Luke 12:29–31

Fasting is a way of asking God to move powerfully in our lives and in our world.

People in the Bible frequently fasted to seek something from God.

> "I [Ezra] proclaimed a fast, so that we might humble ourselves before our God and ask him for a safe journey for us and our children, with all our possessions." —Ezra 8:21

> In the Old Testament, among other reasons, the people of Israel often fasted as they repented and cried out for God's forgiveness. Examples: 1 Samuel 7:6; Jeremiah 36:6, 9; Nehemiah 1:4; Daniel 9:3.

> In the New Testament, we see early Christians fasting for other reasons: For example, in Acts 13:2–3, the prophets and leaders of the church in Antioch fast and pray in order to seek the Lord's guidance on a big decision: who to send out to preach the gospel in the surrounding area. Also, in Acts 14:23, Luke records that Paul and Barnabas fasted and prayed in order to commission and bless the ministry of the people they were sending out.

In each of these instances (and more), God's people fasted in the hope that he would reveal himself in one way or another. Are you facing any big decisions? Do you want to find a good way to bless someone's ministry? Consider a fast!

Examples	Type of Fast	Who's Fasting?
Judges 20:26	Not specified	Israel's soldiers
1 Samuel 7:6	Not specified	The nation of Israel
2 Samuel 12:16–17	No food	David
Nehemiah 1:4	Not specified	Nehemiah
Esther 4:3	Not specified	All Jewish provinces in which King Xerxes' edict of annihilation of the Jewish people was read
Esther 4:15–6	No food, no drink	All of the Jewish people in the city of Susa
Jeremiah 36:6, 9	Not specified	A time of fasting was proclaimed for the nation of Israel.
Daniel 1:8–14	Nothing but vegetables and water	Daniel, Hananiah, Mishael, and Azariah
Daniel 9:3	Not specified	Daniel
Daniel 10:2–3	No "choice" food or drink	Daniel
Joel 1:14; 2:12–15	Not specified	The whole nation of Israel
Jonah 3:5–10	No food, no drink	The people of Nineveh
Matthew 4:2	Not specified	Jesus
Luke 2:37	Not specified	Anna
Acts 9:9	No food, no drink	Paul
Acts 13:2–3	Not specified	The prophets and teachers of the church in Antioch
Acts 14:23	Not specified	Paul and Barnabas

Four Types of Fasts

I t's important to note that Scripture doesn't provide specific instructions on the mechanics of how to fast. There are only a handful of instances in the Bible in which the method being used is even mentioned. Here are four general categories of fasts.

1. No Food, No Drink

Esther calls the people of Israel to an extreme fast in preparation for her meeting with King Xerxes.

> Esther said: "Go, gather together all the Jews who are in Susa, and fast for me. Do not eat or drink for three days, night or day. I and my attendants will fast as you do. When this is done, I will go to the king, even though it is against the law. And if I perish, I perish." — Esther 4:16

Esther's extreme fast was for an extreme situation: she was preparing to break the law by going to the king when not summoned to try to persuade him to prevent the annihilation of her people, the Jews. Extreme fasting is rare; Esther's example, Paul in Acts 9:9, and the people of Nineveh in the book of Jonah are the only times it appears in the Bible.

2. No Food

This type of fast is by far the most common in the Bible. For example:

> ❯ In Judges 20:26 the entire army of Israel "went up to Bethel, and there they sat weeping before the Lord. They fasted that day until evening and presented burnt offerings and fellowship offerings to the Lord." This was a short-term fast in which the Israelites asked for God's guidance and his protection in battle.

> ❯ In Luke 2:37, we see the example of a prophetess named Anna. Luke doesn't elaborate on the type of fast she conducted, but he mentions that she does so frequently: "She never left the temple but worshiped night and day, fasting and praying."

> ❯ Jesus' time in the wilderness shows that fasting should help us remember that we need God more than we need anything else. His responses to each of Satan's temptations show his belief

with your friends or a small group. Try to answer questions such as *How did God reveal himself during my fast?* or *What were the most challenging issues I confronted?* Perhaps what you discover about your fast can encourage others.

My Fast Didn't "Work." What Went Wrong?

Whether you're fasting for very particular reasons, such as guidance on a big decision, or just to grow closer to the Lord, you may be forced to confront the reality of an "unanswered" fast. It can be painful and confusing to realize that the goal you had in mind for your fast isn't transpiring the way you had hoped.

How should you respond? You may be tempted to assume that you didn't execute the fast correctly, or even to think that fasting simply has no value. Resist that temptation! Remember that fasting, like praying, is a process. Our prayer lives often mature when we hear nothing but silence from God. The same can be true for fasting. God may be working behind the scenes or growing us spiritually in ways that we're not yet aware of. In such times, remind yourself that fasting, like the other spiritual disciplines, is ultimately an act of worship toward the Lord.

> One thing I ask from the LORD, this only do I seek: that I may dwell in the house of the LORD all the days of my life, to gaze on the beauty of the LORD and to seek him in his temple. —Psalm 27:4

Also, when we fast, just like when we pray, we should be persistent. Luke 11:5–13 relates the parable of the friend in need. Jesus tells his disciples a story of a man who visits a friend late at night, asking for food. After the friend refuses, Jesus says, "I tell you, even though he will not get up and give you the bread because of friendship, yet because of your shameless audacity he will surely get up and give you as much as you need" (11:8). Jesus encourages us to petition him consistently and with *shameless* audacity.

Lastly, even if we don't receive the things we fast and pray for, we should remember that we often learn more about ourselves and grow closer to God through difficulty and suffering.

> In all this you greatly rejoice, though now for a little while you may have had to suffer grief in all kinds of trials. These have come so that the proven genuineness of your faith—of greater worth than gold, which perishes even though refined by fire—may result in praise, glory and honor when Jesus Christ is revealed. —1 Peter 1:6–7

that God, not ourselves, is the ultimate Sustainer of human life.

> After fasting forty days and forty nights, he was hungry. The tempter came to him and said, "If you are the Son of God, tell these stones to become bread." Jesus answered, "It is written: 'Man shall not live on bread alone, but on every word that comes from the mouth of God.'" —Matthew 4:2–4

Jesus didn't want to break his fast through any means other than what came from the Father. Turning those stones into warm bread would've satisfied Jesus' hunger, but it also would've revealed that he trusted in himself, in his own power, to provide for his needs. He chose instead to trust in the sustaining power of God the Father.

During this type of fast, people choose a specific amount of time during which they abstain from all food. Most people who choose this type of fast for lengthy stretches of time combine it with various juices.

3. The "Daniel Fast"

In the book of Daniel, the prophet fasts, in a couple of different places, by avoiding tasty foods and beverages.

1. Daniel chose not to eat the delicacies afforded to him by his position in King Nebuchadnezzar's palace in order to avoid defiling himself with the food and wine of Judah's conqueror.

> "Please test your servants for ten days: Give us nothing but vegetables to eat and water to drink. Then compare our appearance with that of the young men who eat the royal food, and treat your servants in accordance with what you see." —Daniel 1:12–13

2. Later in the book of Daniel, while in mourning because the people of Israel felt disconnected from God, Daniel decides to fast from anything appetizing.

> "I ate no choice food; no meat or wine touched my lips; and I used no lotions at all until the three weeks were over." —Daniel 10:3

People in Daniel's day didn't have nearly as many food and beverage options as we enjoy today. Consequently, his decision to forego meat and wine meant that he committed himself to an extremely simple, even boring, diet—depriving himself of the pleasure of "choice" foods.

People who choose this type of fast usually refrain from eating anything too flavorful or substantial.

> Rejoice always, pray continually, give thanks in all circumstances; for this is God's will for you in Christ Jesus.
> —1 Thessalonians 5:16–18

Set aside time for God's Word. Be sure to make time to study God's Word. Meditate on its proverbs, remember its counsel, and memorize Christ's words. Praying to God and reading Scripture can offer guidance while we make a tough choice, petition God for something, or just remind us of God's faithfulness, but ultimately, their main purpose is to help us acknowledge God's character—to conform us to his image. Fasting heightens this context. Take in as much of the Bible as possible. You may want to read Psalm 1, Psalm 30, Psalm 104, and Psalm 121.

> Your word is a lamp for my feet, a light on my path. —Psalm 119:105

Seek God's strength in your weakness. When we fast, we place our spiritual needs and our desire to experience the presence of Christ over our physical needs. When we feel weak, our defenses are lowered. Genuine frustrations, anger, bitterness, and discouragement are going to surface much more quickly. We're forced into a level of sincerity when we fast—and doesn't God want us to be honest with ourselves and with him? Fasting can help us get to a sincere place—a context that facilitates growth.

> But he said to me, "My grace is sufficient for you, for my power is made perfect in weakness." Therefore I will boast all the more gladly about my weaknesses, so that Christ's power may rest on me. —2 Corinthians 12:9

After You Fast

Ease yourself back into the things you've avoided. It's important, especially if you've fasted from food for a long period of time, to slowly ease yourself back into your daily meals (don't get two extra-large meals from McDonald's and pig out!). If you completed a non-food fast, hopefully part of the reason you attempted it

was to help you see your time-management from a more Christ-centered perspective (don't make up for lost time by binge-watching your TV shows!).

Reflect on what God showed you during your fast. Fasting can be a powerful way of drawing closer to the Lord. It may be helpful to journal about what you learned during your fast. You could also discuss the experience